EcoZones

SEASHORES

Lynn M. Stone

Photos by Lynn M. Stone

ROURKE ENTERPRISES, INC.
Vero Beach, FL 32964

Library of Congress Cataloging in Publication Data

Stone, Lynn M.
  The sea shore.

  Includes index.
  Summary: Examines the seashore as an ecological niche and describes the plant and animal life supported there.
    1. Seashore biology — Juvenile literature.   2. Seashore ecology — Juvenile literature.   [1. Seashore biology.
2. Seashore ecology.   3. Ecology]   I. Title.
II. Series: Stone, Lynn M.   Ecozones.
QH95.7.S746   1989   574.5'2638   89-10538
ISBN 0-86592-435-X

CONTENTS

THE SEASHORE

To some people, nothing is sweeter than the smell of salt air. It's not that the tang of air laced with ocean breath smells like a rose garden. It's simply that when you smell salt air, you know the seashore is nearby. The seashore is a magical mix of land and ocean—the edge of land, the edge of the sea, and a restless union of both. Perhaps none of the natural communities in North America inspires as much wonder and affection as the seashore.

Pick a beach and plant yourself at the sea's edge, where the tongues of waves lap your feet. Listen to the rhythmic wash of waves and the yelp of gulls. The seashore proper—at least the shore of the moment—is under your feet. But all around you, in a greater sense, is the seashore too—the near offshore water, the sky, the slope of sand or wedge of rock at your back.

Especially in sheltered bays and on rocky coasts, the seashore reveals life exceptionally diverse and plentiful, from seaweeds and sponges to porpoises and eagles. Considerable amounts of seashore life are hidden under the shallow

Opposite *The Pacific coast is a trail of tall bluffs, bays, mountains, rock formations and interludes of sand. Pictured: Boiler Bay State Park, Oregon.*

sea or in the sands, and the narrow corridor between dry land and open ocean is brimming with life, whether it is visible or not. Nature has been astonishingly thorough; there is scarcely a place in the seashore world without life.

The shores are visited daily—most often twice daily—by high tides. The oceans are subject to the effects of winds, tremors in the earth, and gravity—the earth's and also the gravitational pull of the moon and the sun. The earth's natural, whirling movement through space, the influences of gravity, and the slope of any given coast all combine to make the oceans move. The move toward a daily rise of seawater along the shore is called the high tide. After the high water mark is reached, water begins to retreat until low tide is reached. Then the tide begins advancing again.

In some locations, such as Key West, Florida, the difference in tides is relatively small. In other places, tides may cause a great deal of amazement. The Bay of Fundy on Canada's northeastern shores has the greatest tidal variation in the world, over 50 feet. When the tide is out, great, glistening stretches of sea bottom are uncovered. Sister islands that had been separated by deep water can be reached by walking from one to the other.

The tides are water in motion, and moving water is critical for the life of the seashore. The sea brings oxygen and food with its rise and carries away wastes, eggs, and developing forms of **marine** creatures with its wake. For many of the tiny, yet important, creatures of the sea, their only means of transport is the shifting of the tides.

TYPES OF SEASHORE

The tides wash an unimaginable number of different seashores, but despite individual variations they are all composed basically of rock, sand, mud, or coral. The entire coastline of North America, which extends from Alaska, the Canadian Arctic, and Greenland south through Central America, is beyond the scope of this book. We'll confine our seashore exploration to the area between southern British Columbia and the Mexican border on the Pacific and Newfoundland and the Florida Keys on the Atlantic coast.

On the foggy North Atlantic shores, from Newfoundland to Cape Cod, the seaward thumb of Massachusetts, the seashore is generally rock-bound and broken by inlets and coves. A gull's straight line route along the Maine shore from Portland to the Canadian border is about 200 miles. If someone followed each nook of the Maine coast, it would be a 2,500-mile journey.

The pattern and form of the rocks along these shores of Newfoundland, Nova Scotia, Quebec, New Brunswick, Prince Edward Island, and Maine varies

Opposite *Sandy shores, like this one on Florida's west coast, prevail from Cape Cod, Massachusetts, southward.*

widely. The few sandy beaches have a scattering of rock rubble. Some beaches are solidly floored with cobblestones. Most of the northeast coast is strapped by ledges, boulders, and rocky points. There is little margin on most of these beaches between land and sea. Land often ends with **conifers** marching right to the sea's doorstep.

The Atlantic coast south of Cape Cod to southern Florida is essentially sandy, interspersed here and there by bays and salt marshes with their maze of tidal streams. Off the southern tip of Florida lie the Florida Keys. The upper keys, those islands closest to the mainland, are made of coral. The lower keys are limestone rock, much of which is covered by sand.

North of the keys, along the gulf coast from southwestern Florida to Alabama, Mississippi, Louisiana, and Texas, the shore is a checkerboard of sand, salt marsh, and wooded islands.

The Pacific coast from southern California north into southern British Columbia is a breathtaking trail of tall bluffs, bays, mountains, rock formations, and interludes of sand.

Along both the Pacific and Atlantic coasts, the land and sea merge in a remarkable panorama of landscapes.

Open shores are thrashed by waves, but countless other shores are sheltered from the open sea by pickets of rock or the sweep of land extensions. The sea takes many paths to the shore, and many of them are quite roundabout. Look at a detailed map of the North American coasts and notice the many fingers of the sea reaching into and around coves, inlets, islands, and lagoons.

Along the shores are numerous seashore **habitats**. Each habitat is a place where living conditions are different from those somewhere else on the sea-

Above *Along the North Atlantic, the seashore is rockbound and broken by coves and inlets. (Acadia National Park, Maine.)*

SEASHORES

shore. The distance that a shore lies north or south, the temperature of the water, the lay of the land, the effect of the tides and currents, and several other environmental factors have a bearing on the habitats that are available for plants and animals. Even such seemingly minor differences as those created by whether a seaside boulder faces seaward or landward helps determine which plants and animals will live on or under it.

All beaches have fairly clear zones in which certain plants and animals live. When **ecologists**, scientists who study the interrelationships of plants and animals within their environment, look at a seashore, they notice its **zonation**— the way it is naturally divided into zones. In other words, certain plants and animals seem to congregate in a fairly narrow band of the shore, leaving other bands to different plants and animals.

Each seashore habitat varies, but certain kinds of major habitats are more common than others. Sand beaches are usually broad and tapered. The upper-most part of a sandy shore is the dune region. Some of the dunes on the Atlantic coast, built by dry, blowing sands, have grown into miniature mountains 30 to 40 feet tall.

The dune lies above the high tide line by several paces. Under normal conditions, the dune is not flooded by saltwater. Most sand dunes in their natural state are anchored by plants. Animals of the dunes tend to be common land forms: a wealth of insects, spiders, a few snakes, occasional toads, cottontail rabbits, and many other animals that wander onto the dune from neighboring land.

A few steps from the dune, closer to the sea, lies the upper beach zone. This region may be nipped by high tides, but generally remains clear. The highest line of **wrack**, the ocean's ribbon of refuse, collects at the lower edge of the high beach. The comparatively rich plant life of the dune is absent on the high beach because of increasing **salinity**, the level of salt, in the air and sand.

Wrack is a collection of everything the ocean tosses ashore. Such natural objects as seaweed, the egg cases of snails, driftwood, shells, and the bodies of marine animals are typically part of the wrack. Wrack is frequently inspected by gulls, fish crows, and shore birds. Scavenger beetles, beach hoppers, sand fleas, and flies live in the wrack. Ghost crabs, particularly active at night, live in burrows on the upper beach.

Below the upper beach and the wrack is the **intertidal** area. This section of the beach is submerged under high tides and exposed during low tides. When the tide is out, long ripple marks may be scribbled on the intertidal sand. The intertidal is the zone favored by most shore birds. Willets and plovers pick morsels from the wet sand. Sanderlings throw caution to the wind and seem to chase the retreating waves. Their timing has to be perfect. The little, sand-colored birds dash into the waves' wash for a few seconds of probing, then scurry landward as the next wave charges ashore.

The intertidal sand never completely dries out. It is flooded at least once daily by incoming tidal water and, in most cases, twice. The animals that live in this zone depend on considerably more moisture than the ghost crab of the upper beach. The intertidal is home for such animals as mole crabs, ghost shrimp, clams, olive snails, coquinas, burrowing worms, and microscopic animals that live among the grains of sand.

Since many of the animals in the intertidal zone burrow, their signatures on the sand are more familiar than the animals themselves. The glass-smooth olive snail, for instance, leaves a tiny ridge in the sand as it creeps along just under the surface.

Like sandy shores, rocky beaches are also zoned. Just above the high tide line is a region often called the lichen, spray, or black zone. Simple, hardy plants called lichens grow on the rocks here like black smudges. The ocean doesn't quite submerge them but they are frequently sprayed by the churning surf. Just below the lichens is another band, or zone. This is occupied by certain kinds of algae, another of the simple plants. Many insects and crustaceans, little animals with hard,

segmented shells, are active here.

Closer to the sea lies the intertidal zone, which is best observed at low tide. The intertidal zone begins with the appearance of seaweeds, one of the types of algae. One type, rockweed, anchors its stems to rocks and often covers rocks entirely with dark, slippery growth. Periwinkle snails, limpets, and numerous crustaceans live more densely in this zone than in the higher zone.

Still closer to the low tide level is a zone where great concentrations of crusty barnacles live. The lowest intertidal region is the most intriguing because it has marine organisms in greater abundance than in the drier intertidal zones. The lower intertidal animals vary from one coastal location to the next, but sea urchins, several **species** of crabs, sea anemones, mussels, barnacles, and sea stars (starfish) occur along most rocky shores.

This zone is exposed only during the lowest tides, but so rich is its marine life that experienced tide poolers plan their visits around these extremely low tides. Tide pools are usually found in depressions in rocks. When the tide flows out, the tide pools retain seawater and colorful wall-to-wall marine creatures.

Tide pools, especially on the Pacific coast, are exciting habitats for anyone who wants to observe intertidal life at arm's reach. One exceptional site to explore tide pool life is the Marine Gardens Shore Preserve, an area of extensive rocks and tidal pools near Depoe Bay, Oregon. You can walk—carefully to be sure—from one slick rock to another and inspect clear pools lined with giant green anemones, coral leaf seaweed, balloon-like sea sacs, purple and orange ochre sea stars, purple urchins, great clusters of midnight blue mussels, numerous snails, and several other animals and plants of the Pacific shore.

Above *Oregon tidepool lined with giant green anemone, purple sea urchins, and algae.*

Muddy shores are a feature of bays and other places protected from the roaring surf of open ocean. Muddy shores are found on both coasts, but they are more numerous along the Atlantic and the Gulf of Mexico than on the Pacific coast.

One of the most important muddy regions of the eastern coasts is the salt marsh. Salt marshes often develop near **estuaries**, the junction of river and ocean. Rivers carry soil with their current, but the ocean's flow against the river forces much of the soil to be deposited at the river's mouth, where extensions of the mainland—and salt marshes—are formed.

The salt marsh supports plants such as cattails and *Spartina* grass. Since a salt marsh is at the ocean's door, it is periodically flooded by ocean tides. The tides transport a rich **detritus**—nutritious pieces and particles of decaying marsh plants—to the sea. Incoming tides carry oxygen and marine organisms into the twisting tidal rivers of the marshes.

Like other shores, salt marshes have zones. As the level of ground rises, the marsh grasses that can tolerate salt-water flooding yield to plants such as pickle weed. Pickle weed and various

sedges can live in salty mud, but they cannot be bathed regularly in saltwater.

The mud of salt marshes is a home for such animals as fiddler crabs, clams, oysters, worms, marsh snails, and mussels. The sea hare, shrimp, and a multitude of fish are among the marine animals that slip into the marshes on advancing tides.

Another muddy habitat of the shore is the mangrove swamp. Although mangrove trees live in many tropical and subtropical locations, they occur in the United States only along the southern shores of Florida. Like the salt marshes, mangrove swamps contribute tons of detritus to the coastal habitats while helping to stabilize bay bottoms against ocean tides and currents.

Above *Salt marshes punctuate both coasts, but they are much more plentiful in the East. This marsh is in South Carolina.*

MAKING OF THE SEASHORE

The many variations of North American seashores represent the work of numerous natural forces. Many of the forces that shaped the coasts are still in business, guaranteeing that shorelines will be continually changing. When compared to today's coastline maps, maps drawn by sixteenth-century British and Spanish explorers show how dramatically the American shoreline has changed in the last 400 years.

One of the forces that acts most quickly to change the shore's substance is a storm. Storms, along with frequent winds and tides, are largely responsible for having created the sea islands of Virginia, the Carolinas, and Georgia. The same forces could eventually wear the islands away.

Elsewhere, the **geologic** events that lifted the earth's crust and created seaside mountains shaped much of the Pacific coast. Waves have eroded the softer rocks of the uplifted land, leaving harder rocks called **sea stacks** standing like gates and pillars in the surf.

In the North Atlantic, the crusty shoreline and its intricate network of

coves and islands is largely the product of **glaciation**. The last **glaciers** here melted some 14,000 years ago. The water locked up in these mighty, frozen fortresses of ice and snow poured into the sea, raising the sea level about 400 feet. What had formerly been land, already lowered and gouged by the weight of the glaciers, was flooded. Seawater swept around hills and turned them into islands. Maine alone has over 1,000 coastal islands that are the remains of what was once dry land.

Above Sea stacks remain along Oregon coast and other Pacific shores after softer coastal rocks erode away.

21

The changing lines of seashores from north Florida and along the gulf coast into Texas are largely a result of rivers. As soil deposits build in estuaries, the river flow simply finds another path to the sea. The deposits of soil left by the river are collectively called the delta. Deltas are in constant change as storms and river courses shift earth and water.

The upper keys of the Florida Keys are actually the work of corals, small, soft-bodied animals of warm seas. Corals secrete a hard lime in more or less a tube shape. The tubes give their builders protection, and the sea currents deliver a steady flow of food. As neighboring corals build their lime tubes next to each other, the entire cluster becomes a fused coral reef, one of the most fascinating and colorful marine habitats.

Florida's upper keys, from Sand Key to Loggerhead Key, are ancient coral reefs. When the ocean level subsided thousands of years ago the coral reefs were exposed. What had been living reefs died. Fortunately, there are other spectacular living reefs near the upper and lower keys.

PLANTS
OF THE SEASHORE

4

If we take the plants of seaside dunes, fields, and forests into account, the plants of the seashore are indeed numerous. Just about any plant that grows within the influence of the sea can be loosely considered a seashore plant. That would include the plants of the tidal zones as well as the land plants that are not in direct contact with tidal waters but are still affected by the sea wind, salt, moisture, and spray.

Many plants that aren't normally associated with the shore nevertheless grow there. The great spruce forests of the Northwest and the North Atlantic coasts are an example. In the Southeast, cabbage palms, some pines, and snarls of bayberry grow on the sand dunes. On the southern California coast, rare, wind-twisted torrey pines are protected in a state reserve on the sandy bluffs near La Jolla. Another California rarity is the stately Monterey cypress, which seems to thrive on the wind and spray of the Monterey Peninsula.

Hundreds of flowering plants brighten the shores of both coasts. Among the most conspicuous on the

Right *A dune at Ano Nuevo, California, sports yellow tree-lupine and succulent sea figs.*

Right *The rockweed family of seaweeds is common on both coasts in the intertidal zone.*

east coast are wild roses, coreopsis, beach plum, and sea grape. Beach morning glories, several beach peas, and sandspurs are common to both coasts. On the Pacific coast, seaside daisies wave over oceanside bluffs. Yellow sand verbena huddle in low dunes. Tree lupines, tall, yellow-blossomed shrubs that sometimes reach six feet in height, rise on high dunes. Various **succulents**, plants that store water in their leaves, thrive in the mists that blow over Pacific rocks and bluffs.

The most common plants of the sea itself are diatoms. They are, in fact, the most abundant plants in the world. But you've never seen a diatom; they are microscopic.

Diatoms are perhaps the most important plants of the seashore as well as the most numerous. They make up much of the sea's **plankton** mass. Plankton refers to the millions of tiny plants and animals that swim or float near the surface of the sea.

You cannot see diatoms, but you can't miss seeing the large algae. Hundreds of algae species live in the sea and in the intertidal zone. Most of them are seaweeds. Their ribbon and branch-like forms are hiding places and food for several marine animals. The giant kelp of California is a seaweed that can grow to 300 feet in length. Imagine a strand of seaweed that is the length of a football field! Sea otters wrap themselves in the floating ribbons of giant kelp to enhance their buoyancy while they snooze.

Sea grasses grow in submerged, green jungles, often close to land. Their waving leaves are a haven for fish, crabs, snails, urchins, shrimp, and a swarm of other animals. Few animals graze directly on the marine grasses, but their detritus is a source of food for many animals.

SEASHORE ANIMALS

There may be no better place than a rocky shore at low tide to study the animal kingdom. You can't see the simplest microscopic animals, the one-celled protozoans. You can, however, see animals from many other major groups.

There are sponges, for example, from the group Porifera. Sponges resemble plants, but they are animals equipped with holes and chambers for the circulation of water and food.

Slightly more advanced in the animal world are the coelenterates, most of them looking like a hollow sac pro-tected by tentacles. The tentacles con-tain a toxin, or poison, that they use to capture prey. Jellyfish and sea anemones are both among the 9,000-plus species of coelenterates.

The annelids are represented by three groups of worms—flat, ribbon, and segmented. The arthropods are creatures with jointed legs. Insects are arthropods, and so are crustaceans. Crustaceans have hard shells and paired groups of legs or similar **appendages**. Lobsters and the many crab species are crustaceans.

Opposite Atlantic *puffins carry fish back to their nest burrows on rocky Canadian shores after dives into the open sea.*

Above *Ghost crabs live in burrows on upper beach just above high tide line from New Jersey south.*

The horseshoe crab of the Atlantic coast is not a crab, but it is an arthropod and a relative of the spider. Scientists say that the horseshoe crab has remained almost entirely unchanged for 150 million years.

Without sand dollars, sea urchins, and sea stars—echinoderms all—the seashore would not be the same. Echinoderms are animals with spiny skins, and they are truly marine animals. None of the 5,000 or so species of echinoderms lives on land or in freshwater.

Certain mollusks would be safer if there were no echinoderms. Sea stars feed on several mollusks, but many of the mollusks feed upon each other, too. The crown conch and tulip snails of the Southeast frequently prey on clams, oysters, and other sea snails.

Mollusks are animals that typically have hard shells—clams, snails, oysters, mussels, and the like. A few, such as the sea hare, octopus, and squid, have only internal remnants of shells. They have the characteristic soft bodies of mollusks, but they have uncharacteristic protection—a cloud of toxic fluid is released when they feel threatened.

One of the most prized mollusks is abalone. Abalone shells are rough on the outside, but the inside is a gleaming pearl color. The meat of some species of abalone from the California coast is very valuable.

Another West Coast mollusk of some stature is the goeduck clam. Goeducks may weigh up to 20 pounds and have a siphon, or breathing tube, 24 inches long.

Mollusks are the reason that many people comb beaches, although a person probably won't say, "I'm hunting for mollusks." More likely, the beachcomber will say, "I'm looking for shells." Of course, shells *are* mollusks, and they seem to have no end of shape and color. Their beauty has inspired people all over the globe to collect shells. Unfortunately, collecting live shells has contributed to the scarcity of many species of marine mollusks.

To this point, we have only been considering animals without a backbone, **invertebrates**. The usually larger, more intelligent, and more structurally advanced animals are **vertebrates**, animals with backbones. These include fish, amphibians, reptiles, birds, and mammals.

Amphibians—frogs, salamanders, and toads—do not live in or very close to seawater, although toads occasionally appear on dunes. The variety of reptiles along the shores is a bit greater. Snakes live in the scrubby vegetation of dunes and marshes, and small numbers of American crocodiles live in the salty lagoons and creeks of the upper Florida Keys and Everglades National Park at the tip of the Florida peninsula. Diamondback terrapins are found in salt marshes from Massachusetts to Texas. The major reptilian attraction of the shores is the loggerhead turtle, normally found from North Carolina south to the Florida coasts.

The loggerhead is one of several sea turtle species, but it is the only one that nests regularly in the United States. Loggerheads only come ashore to dig their nest holes. They lay approximately 120 golfball-sized eggs in a sandy nest hole. Each female may nest several times during the season, which begins in May and continues into August. After nesting, the 300-pound loggerhead crawls back into the sea.

Although the turtle arrives at night, her presence often draws the attention of raccoons, which dig up her eggs. Her nest also faces destruction from storms. When the turtles hatch, they may be attacked and eaten by raccoons, herons, ghost crabs, and—if they reach the sea—large fish.

Below *A loggerhead sea turtle at dune's edge covers her nest before returning to the Gulf of Mexico.*

Many species of saltwater fish, large and small, spend all or part of their life cycles in coastal waters. The sheltered waters—bays, marshes, swamps, lagoons, creeks—are extremely important nurseries for young fish. Even large, predatory fish, however, are part of the intertidal zone.

Along much of the Pacific shore and in the rocky coves of the Northeast, seals can be seen bobbing in the waves or sunning on rocks. Harbor seals are the most common seals in the coastal waters of the Northeast. The much less common gray seals of the Northeast are almost twice the length—nearly 10 feet—of harbor seals.

California sea lions, the much larger Steller's sea lions, harbor seals, and the giant northern elephant seals live along the Pacific seashore. The most spectacular of the four species is the elephant seal, named for the drooping, inflatable snout that looks somewhat elephantlike, especially on such a huge body. Males can exceed 21 feet in length, and author Sheri Howe described them in *Mirounga,* her book about elephant seals, as "three ton mountains of fat."

Northern elephant seals were nearly wiped out in the late 1800s by seal hunters. Their hides were valuable, and their blubber, or fat, was boiled into oil. An adult male elephant seal could provide 200 gallons of high quality oil for street lighting, machinery lubrication, soap production, waterproof clothing, and paint.

With protection from both the United States and Mexico, the elephant seals rebounded. There are now over 100,000 northern elephant seals. They rest and breed on sandy shores, usually on offshore islands.

Another sea mammal that has made a comeback from near-extinction is the sea otter. Sea otters disappeared from the California coast for almost 100 years. The animals reappeared off Carmel, California, in 1938, and their numbers gradually climbed to around 1,000. Sea otters are more plentiful in Alaskan waters.

Sea otters rarely swim ashore, but they hunt abalone, sea urchins, crabs, and other sea food close to land. Seashore visitors in the vicinity of Carmel and Monterey can always find sea otters. In fact, sea otter-watching is a major attraction because of the otters' fascinating eating habits. They are one of the few animals to use "tools." Sea otters frequently crack shellfish against

Right *Once hunted nearly to extinction for their thick, lustrous pelts, California sea otters have made a comeback along the central coast.*

Right *One of the most intelligent of sea creatures, the bottle-nosed dolphin (porpoise) occurs on both coasts.*

a rock held tightly to their chests. They typically swim on their backs and use their chests as tables.

Sea otters may have the finest fur of any mammal. Exceptionally thick and lustrous, it does a superb job of keeping the sea otters warm. Unfortunately, in the past the sea otters' coats made them the target of intense hunting. An international treaty in 1911 stopped the slaughter, but by then the otters had nearly vanished.

Pacific coast watchers often see the barnacle-encrusted hides of gray whales rise and fall as they swim toward Baja California or north toward the Arctic seas. Watchers on both coasts also see dolphins, small whales that are also called porpoises.

The birds of the seashores that we "know"—shore birds and gulls—are the ones we see most often. Many birds of the shores are less familiar because they live there only during part of the year or live on rugged cliffs almost beyond view.

For the most part, the birds of the seashore are fish-eaters. Perhaps the most impressive of the lot are two birds of prey, the osprey (fish hawk) and bald eagle. Both birds build huge nests of sticks in trees or on cliffs, and both dive from great heights to snare fish that are swimming near the surface.

Another remarkable fisherman is the brown pelican of California and the Southeast. While the osprey and eagle use their talons to clutch prey, the brown pelican dives headlong into the sea and grabs fish in its bill. Their relatives, the white pelicans, which winter along the coasts of Mexico, California, Texas, and Florida, have a different technique. They fish by swimming in a semicircle, herding fish ahead of them. As the pelicans tighten the circle, they use their "dip net" pouches to scoop up fish.

Some of the other well-known fish-eating birds of the seashore are terns, loons, grebes, cormorants, herons and egrets, and several kinds of ducks. Fish-eating gannets, murres, guillemots, and puffins live on high, rocky ledges and do some of their fishing far from shore.

Just as the pelican species fill separate **niches**, or roles, in the seashore environment, so do the other fishing birds. The pelican species rarely fish together or compete since each has a different style and habitat. The brown pelican usually fishes in the open sea. The white pelican likes sheltered, still water. The cormorant shares nesting space with the pelicans, but not fishing space. Pelicans grab fish close to the surface; cormorants dive to considerable depths. Herons, depending upon the species and size, spear fish in various depths of seawater.

The seashore birds that don't fish still depend on the ocean for food. Petrels, which nest in seaside burrows, eat plankton from the ocean swells. White ibis, roseate spoonbills, and the shore birds, or sandpipers, eat a variety

Left *High-diving brown pelicans live along coasts of California, Oregon, and the Southeast.*

Left *Sanderlings frequent both coasts, where they dodge surf to feed on tiny invertebrates.*

of little invertebrates.

Many of the ducks eat marine plants or shellfish. Wild geese, brant, and tundra swans eat marine plants. Fish crows, vultures, and gulls scavenge the shores for dead fish and other animal remains. Gulls are also adept at catching live fish.

Above the beach, on the dunes or at the forest edge, the bird life reflects whatever species are characteristic of the area, from woodpeckers and doves to various warblers.

6 THE FLOW OF ENERGY

Like other communities of living things, the shore communities form living **ecosystems**. Plants and animals interrelate with each other in such a way that energy, which enables all living organisms to function, flows from one to another in a somewhat efficient, systematic way. Animals on the shore are there because they function as part of a coastal system, at least during part of their life cycle.

The force behind the energy of coastal communities—dune, intertidal, subtidal, and so forth—is the sun. Plants use sunlight in their food-making process, called **photosynthesis**. Since they manufacture, or produce, food, plants are the bridge between sunlight and animals. Unlike plants, animals aren't **producers**; they do not manufacture food from sunlight and the basic elements of life contained in air, water, and soil. Instead, plants manufacture food, and animals are **consumers**. In one way or another, they consume the energy originally stored in the plants.

The most basic plants of the seashore are the microscopic plant plank-

Opposite *Osprey, grasping flounder from a Florida bay, will take food energy from the fish, which had previously taken it from smaller animals.*

ton. These are eaten by animal plankton and other, larger animals, which, in turn, are consumed by still larger creatures. Throughout the seashore community, there are plant-eating animals, **herbivores**, and meat-eating animals, **carnivores**. Many herbivores become food for carnivores, but small carnivores themselves become food for larger carnivores. The largest, most powerful carnivores, like ospreys and elephant seals, are not eaten by other animals.

The path of energy from producer to animal consumer can be very complex, or it can be quite straightforward. Whatever twists the flow of energy takes as it passes from a plant to an animal is called a food chain. A typical seashore food chain begins with plankton. A small fish consumes thousands of plankton animals and plants and becomes, itself, prey for a larger fish. The larger fish, perhaps four inches in length, is grabbed by a gleaming sea trout about 16 inches long.

The carnivorous trout is one of the larger fishes in the forest of turtle grass where it lives at high tide. Few other fish in the bay are large enough to snack on the trout. But as the trout's silvery back flashes near the surface, it is sighted by an osprey. Wings cocked, then folded, the osprey rockets downward. The sea trout, still twisting in the bird's talons, is soon being eaten on the osprey's feeding perch.

Throughout the chain, energy is being passed—from sunlight and detritus to plankton, from plankton to fish, and finally to the osprey. Each consumer in the chain is nourished by some of the energy stored in its prey. Ultimately, the osprey becomes feeble in old age and loses its ability to catch fish. In death, the osprey is eaten by **decomposers**. They consist mostly of **bacteria** which eventually reduce the osprey to particles that can be absorbed by air, water, and soil. Now, the energy once stored in the osprey—some of the same energy once stored in the sun and plankton—returns to the environment where it can be used by plants once again.

7 CONSERVATION OF THE SEASHORE

Shoreline land has become extremely popular and increasingly valuable. The beauty and lure of the ocean and the need for seaside ports have resulted in tremendous pressures on seashores. Some of the largest population centers—Boston, New York, Philadelphia, Los Angeles, and San Francisco among them—developed on seashores.

The native Indians who lived along the coasts did not destroy the shores. Rather, they became part of them, using the shores' resources for their survival. The Indian cultures, however, were overwhelmed by European culture after the European settlement of North America began in earnest in the seventeenth century. The development of the seashore for housing, industry, recreation, and transportation went unchecked. In recent years, many states have created laws to protect seashores and salt marshes from damaging development. One of the foremost protectors of its oceanfront has been the state of Oregon. While California, its neighbor to the south, turned much of its southern coastline and estuaries over to development,

Opposite *Northern elephant seals, loafing on a protected California beach, have come back from near extinction.*

Oregon salted away almost its entire coast in a chain of state parks and national forests.

Florida has also joined the ranks of states eager to protect shores that were once easy prey for development. Likewise, voters in Maine defeated a plan that would have converted part of the state's scenic shoreline into an oil-processing site.

Not all the shoreline that still remains free of tall buildings and other development will remain that way. Even where building occurs, though, it is usually being done with more care today than in the past. Where beach visitors used to trample dunes in their rush to the surf, many states have erected boardwalks to protect plants.

Meanwhile, shores face other threats: chemical pollutants, trash, and oil spills. Oil may turn out to be the greatest threat. It retains its poisonous characteristics for months, and the oil itself may take years to disappear once it has been released into the sea.

When the *Exxon Valdez*, an oil tanker, ran aground off Alaska in 1989, over 11 million gallons of oil gushed into the sea. A massive oil slick was carried by the sea to shores. Sea otters and birds were trapped in the oil. Beaches and rocks were lathered in oil. The immediate destruction was obvious, but its long-term environmental effects may be felt in the food chains for decades.

The North American seashores are living treasures, abundantly rich in beauty and life. In that way, they are like fine sea shells. We need to remember that they are like fine sea shells in another way, also—they are fragile.

GLOSSARY

appendage a limb or extension of the body

bacteria a class of microscopic plants

carnivore a meat-eating animal

conifer a plant that bears seeds in cones, especially needle-leaved trees

consumer an animal, so named because it must eat, or consume, to live

decomposer an organism, most often bacteria and fungi, that consumes dead tissue and reduces it to small particles

detritus tiny particles of decaying remains of plants and animals

ecologist a scientist who studies the interrelationships of plants and animals in association with their environment

ecosystem a system of exchanges of food and energy between plants and animals and their environment

estuary the portion of a river affected by the rise and fall of tides and where freshwater and saltwater mix

geologic relating to the history of the earth and the rocks of which it is composed

glaciation the process by which glaciers affect the land

glacier a massive river of ice that forms on high ground when snowfall exceeds summer melting

habitat an animal's or plant's immediate surroundings; its specific place within the community

herbivore plant-eating animal

intertidal the coastal area alternately covered by ocean water during high tide and exposed during low tide

invertebrate an animal without a backbone

marine of or related to the ocean

niche an organism's role or job in the community

photosynthesis the process by which green plants produce simple food sugars through the use of sunlight and chlorophyll

plankton the tiny plants and animals that swim or float near the surface of a body of water

producer a green plant, so named for its ability to manufacture, or produce, food

salinity the level of salt in a medium such as water

sea stack a towering rock formation projecting from the sea

segmented separated into parts or sections of a continuous whole

species a group of plants or animals whose members reproduce naturally only with other animals or plants of the same group; a particular kind of plant or animal, such as a bald eagle or ochre sea star

succulent a fleshy plant that stores liquid in its stems or leaves

vertebrate an animal with a backbone

wrack the line of sea refuse that marks the highest reach of the tide

zonation a natural organization of plant associations in more or less parallel bands arranged as a consequence of variations in environmental conditions

SEASHORE SITES

The following is a sampling of outstanding sites where you can expect to find characteristic plants and animals and seashore scenery:

CANADA

British Columbia
Pacific Rim National Park, Ucluelet, British Columbia
New Brunswick
Fundy National Park, Alma, New Brunswick
Prince Edward Island
Prince Edward Island National Park, Charlottetown, Prince Edward Island

UNITED STATES

California
Point Lobos State Reserve, Carmel, California
Point Reyes National Seashore, Point Reyes, California
Florida
Canaveral National Seashore, Titusville, Florida
Gulf Islands National Seashore, Gulf Breeze, Florida
John Pennekamp Coral Reef State Park, Key Largo, Florida
Maryland
Assateague Island National Seashore, Berlin, Maryland
Massachusetts
Cape Cod National Seashore, Eastham, Massachusetts
Maine
Acadia National Park, Bar Harbor, Maine
New Jersey
Brigantine National Wildlife Refuge, Oceanville, New Jersey
North Carolina
Cape Hatteras National Seashore, Manteo, North Carolina
Texas
Padre Island National Seashore, Corpus Christi, Texas

ACTIVITIES

Here are some activities and projects that will help you learn more about the North American seashores:

1. If you live near a shore, make a point to visit it and make observations of the plants and animals that you recognize. Use a camera, notebook, or sketchbook to aid your observation. Write a report in which you explain some of the relationships between the plants and animals that you observed. A library will help you in your research.
2. Design a travel brochure for a particular seashore region. Describe the area's plants, animals, and scenic value. Tell what clothes would be appropriate and why. Tell how to reach the area and how someone would get around once there. Why would people want to go there? What would they be able to do there?
3. Choose one of the animal groups, such as echinoderms, mollusks, crustaceans, or birds, and find out more about some of the seashore-loving members of that group. Explain how they have special characteristics (adaptations) for life in or near saltwater.
4. Join a conservation organization that promotes the protection of seashore plants, animals, and environments. Several national and international organizations are listed here:

UNITED STATES
National Audubon Society
Membership Data Center
P.O. Box 2666
Boulder, CO 80322

National Wildlife Federation
1412 Sixteenth St., NW
Washington, DC 20036

The Sierra Club
730 Polk St.
San Francisco, CA 94109

CANADA
Canadian Nature Federation
75 Albert St., Suite 203
Ottawa, Ontario K1P 9Z9

INDEX

Numbers in boldface type refer to photo pages.